I0453782

IN

LOVE

WITH THE

SUN

SPIRITUAL MESSAGES FROM GODDESS

GAIA

Videotaped January 2, 2013
Happy Science General Headquarters, Tokyo

RYUHO OKAWA
IRH Press

Contents

4
The Mission of Gaia

5
The Speculations
Of Extraterrestrials

6
Gaia's Origin of Soul

7
The Work of Creation on Earth

8
The Guiding Concept of Earth

9
The Meaning of El Cantare's Descent

Preface

I believe this is a book that firmly declares the beginning of New Genesis. While reflecting back on the true Genesis of the human race in the past, the book offers clear guidance to the people of the present day. This book indicates that the dawn of a new civilization is approaching and that the starting point of the future is here in the present moment.

While strongly sympathizing with the heart hidden in the spiritual message from Gaia called "In Love with the Sun," I was moved very deeply by the fact that Alpha and Gaia must work together, hand in hand, to create a new civilization on Earth – such is this book. I would like for you to listen to the bell ringing the advent of a spiritual revolution.

Lord Ryuho Okawa
(Master and CEO of the Happy Science Group)
January 10, 2013

Gaia

When the core part of El Cantare (Fundamental Buddha), Supreme God of the Earth, descended to earth for the first time more than three hundred and dozens of millions of years ago, He took on the name, 'Alpha.' [Refer to *The Laws of Alpha* (Tokyo: Happy Science, 2014)]. Goddess Gaia was the wife of Alpha. From the ancient times, this "cosmic consciousness" has had a role of a helper in El Cantare's creation, and is also called "El Cantare's right hand" [Refer to Chapter 2 in *Jinruisozo no Himitsu ni Semaru* (Closing in on the Secret Behind the Creation of Humankind) (Tokyo: IRH Press, 2013)]. Furthermore, Gaia is now born and living in current Japan as Ryuho Okawa's wife, Shio Okawa.

Interviewer from Happy Science:[*]

Shio Okawa
Aide to Master & CEO

The opinions of the spirits do not necessarily reflect those of Happy Science Group.

[*] The interviewer's professional title represents the position at the time of the interview.

11

1

A New Genesis

Getting new information
In the age of Alpha

RYUHO OKAWA:

I would like to bring up 'Genesis' since it was a suggested topic for the first lecture of the year. When I taught about the laws of Alpha [see page 10], I mentioned a being called 'Gaia.' Today, I am going to record the spiritual messages from Goddess Gaia. The content of today's lecture will probably partially correspond with some part of the Book of Genesis in the Old Testament. Although I can't do it all at once, perhaps it would be better to give some lectures on this kind of topic occasionally.

Today's title, "In Love with the Sun," is a little odd but I wasn't the one who came up with the title; it came from "above." So please don't think that I have suddenly lost my mind. [*Laughs.*] The title which sounds a bit Latin American was given from Heaven. I wonder how today's lecture will turn out to be. Whatever will be, will be.

I have preached about the laws of Alpha, but I have yet to talk about the laws of Gaia. Today, I will summon Gaia to verify the laws of Alpha or to find out how Gaia sees Alpha. I hope we will acquire new knowledge about the age of Alpha or the time of Genesis.

Summoning Gaia,
The spirit that was on earth with Alpha

RYUHO OKAWA:

Let's begin. Are you ready? [*To Shio Okawa.*]

[*Puts hands together and closes eyes.*]

As the first lecture for the year 2013, we will record the spiritual messages from Gaia, who descended to earth with Alpha at the time of Genesis.

[*Puts hands forward with palms facing up, moving them up, down, and sideways.*]

Oh Gaia, Gaia, Gaia, Gaia...
Oh Gaia, Gaia, Gaia, Gaia...
Come down to Happy Science General Headquarters
And reveal to us your presence and thoughts.
Oh Gaia, Gaia, Gaia, Gaia, Gaia...
Oh Gaia, Gaia, Gaia, Gaia...
Gaia, who was on earth with Alpha.
Gaia, who lived in the time of Alpha.
Please come down to General Headquarters and reveal your thoughts to us.

[Moves hands in an inward, circular motion 5 times. Then forms a shape of a mountain with fingertips. About 30 seconds of silence.]

2

Gaia Appears
And Explains Her Existence

Gaia was with Alpha
From the beginning

GAIA:

I am Gaia.

SHIO OKAWA:

Thank you for giving us this opportunity today. I have
heard that you lived in the same era as Alpha. Could
you tell us what kind of position you were born into
and how you met Alpha at that time?

GAIA:

I was there from the beginning.

I don't know why or how, but I just existed.

For some reason I was there from the beginning.

I was not a "created being."

I was already there with Alpha.

Alpha and Gaia
Can only be described as light

SHIO OKAWA:

I understand that Alpha was the Fundamental Buddha's first descent to earth in a physical body. Is it OK to think that you also descended to earth in a physical body?

GAIA:

Was it a physical body? Now that you mention it, it didn't feel like a corporeal body. How can I describe it? It was the light that shined from a corner of Heaven to brighten the earth. It was the light that illuminated the earth from above. It is described as a personification of that light. The existences of Alpha and myself as Gaia appeared as an effect arising from the creative function of light. It was the power that tried to create; that power itself. It was the 'thought' itself. Therefore, my true form is light.

SHIO OKAWA:

When Master Okawa did a space-people reading on me before, while it may have been metaphoric, I heard that your appearance in Alpha's time was like that of a Sphinx. Alpha, himself, was described in a way that was similar to the portrayal of Jesus Christ in the New Testament. The Apocalypse portrays him in Heaven, with glistening eyes and sharp teeth. Could you give us a description of Alpha's actual appearance?

GAIA:

It sounds like an attempt to describe us in a way that humans can understand.

I suppose we would resemble those things if someone had to give their impressions of us. However, the only way to describe us is that we were light itself. Then, I think you could say that those images portray, in a way, the character and quality of our light.

3

Alpha As Seen from Gaia

Alpha was the sun itself that had descended To earth, as well as the source of life

SHIO OKAWA:

We would be grateful if you could tell us about Alpha. Exactly what was Alpha's work here on earth?

GAIA:

You would be mistaken if you assume that we lived like Adam and Eve, or Abraham. I feel that Alpha was the sun itself that had descended to earth. He was the source of energy for all living creatures.

Is it hard to understand what I mean by, "He was the sun that descended to earth"?

You know *The Laws of the Sun*, right?

SHIO OKAWA:

Yes.

GAIA:

So, Alpha is the sun. He is the sun. He is the source of life.

Alpha and Gaia did not have 'parents'

SHIO OKAWA:

Also, in relation to Alpha, we have heard that Alpha descended at a time when various beings from outer space had arrived on Earth and people were in some kind of war for supremacy. Alpha taught people so they could live together in harmony as fellow earthlings. Could you tell us about the time when Alpha was alive on earth?

GAIA:

The universe has always been populated with many people. Looking back at how things were 600 million[*] years ago, I suppose there were many space people who came to see and explore the Earth. However, whether

---

[*] El Miore, the predecessor of El Cantare, started to devise a plan to create a higher humanity on Earth after finishing the experiments on Venusian civilizations. This was 600 million years ago. Refer to *The Laws of Alpha* [as already cited] and Chapter 1 in *The Laws of the Sun* (New York: IRH Press, 2018).

these people could live on Earth was an experiment of sorts, a process of trial and error.

At the time, Earth was already lush with vegetation and many different animal species were emerging. There were a number of groups from outer space who came to Earth with an interest in making it their home.

At that time, there were a group of souls in Heaven that had been brought over from Venus by El Miore in an attempt to conduct a new creation. He intended to create life on Earth mainly from these souls.

In order to directly guide beings in the third dimension, El Miore manifested Himself in a form that was visible to others. I think this was Alpha.

For some reason, I, too, was there at the time but I don't think I had any parents. Although I did not have parents, I was there somehow. I am guessing that El Miore's mission itself manifested and appeared [as Gaia] on this Earth.

4

The Mission of Gaia

I protected Alpha
And helped Him create humankind

SHIO OKAWA:

What was the mission of Gaia? Please tell us.

GAIA:

My mission was to help and protect Alpha. In addition to this, my mission was to create and multiply humankind on earth.

I taught the first humans about the code of
Conduct and the principle of governance

SHIO OKAWA:

Did Gaia's soul have a unique character or feature?

GAIA:

Well, Alpha's central thought is 'creation.' I believe creation or the act of creating was His main raison d'etre. The spirit group of Venus transferred over to Earth as an enormous ball of spiritual life. In other words, many individual souls merged into one gigantic sphere, like a globe, and were moved to Earth. One of Alpha's tasks was to create the first "chosen people" from the Venusian spirit group in Heaven.

This task included the creation of the first human spirits on earth and their incarnation, in other words, the emergence of their physical bodies.

There was also a need to create a code of conduct for them and to teach them the meaning and purpose of life, the work they need to do as human beings and the principle of governance when their numbers grow.

In the beginning, I believe that there was a process of trial and error during the creation of a form that would suit the Earth's environment. My roles were to help in the creation and to establish order until the created beings could do this themselves. When there were those who fell out of line, I sometimes gave instructions to those who had done so.

It was also my job to keep my eye on the animals that already lived on Earth and beings from outer space to prevent them from doing any harm to Alpha while he was on earth.

5

The Speculations of Extraterrestrials

SHIO OKAWA:

You said that one of your jobs was to protect Alpha from being harmed by space beings. Could you tell me what actually happened?

GAIA:

Some space beings with ulterior motives approached the living creatures on Earth, which were still in the midst of evolving to adapt to Earth's environment.

For example, some space beings saw the living creatures on Earth as a source of food. Others came from outer space hoping to make their souls reside in the physical bodies on Earth. However, we could not allow them to do as they wished because we needed to create a feature particular to the spirit group on Earth.

To bring up a story of a long time ago, the Book of Genesis in the Old Testament describes how God created

Heaven and earth in the first six days and then rested on the seventh. This was probably written symbolically through a revelation from Heaven.

Alpha appeared as the Creator and the Master Maker. His mission was a mission accompanied by difficulties.

6

Gaia's Origin of Soul

My true form is a body of energy
That flows within the cosmic tree

SHIO OKAWA:

You have stood by Alpha's side and helped in his work. What kind of characteristic does your soul have? We would be grateful if you could tell us. Recently, we discovered the fact that many people came from outer space, have their origin elsewhere, and are living today as humans on Earth. Could you tell us the origin of your soul?

GAIA:

Not enough has been revealed about reincarnation that happens on a cosmic scale. It is not easy to teach this, as it is very difficult to fix the coordinates of time and space. Stories will cross and become entangled. In that sense, you will find out that there are many errors in what you are told. Also, you need to be aware that their memory is becoming quite vague since it is of something that happened a long time ago.

However, I don't think I was a so-called "soul from outer space." If I were to refer to a law that has already been revealed, I think I would be "a body of energy that flows within the cosmic tree*, the tree of universal life."

So, while there may have been moments when I was incarnated into or took on a physical body out of necessity, I am not an existence that has gone through reincarnation as a space being.

There is a cosmic tree, the branches of which extend into various galaxies. I was the energy flowing in the cosmic tree. If it is difficult for you to conceive of me as a body of energy, you can think of me as being like the tree sap.

---

* The cosmic tree [universal tree of life]: In the ancient myths around the world, there is a legend of an enormous "tree of life" that extends its branches out to the entire universe. This gigantic tree is believed to be the source of all life. Refer to Chapter 5 in Ryuho Okawa, *The Laws of Courage* (New York: IRH Press, 2009).

Alpha holds time and space
Like a ball in each hand

GAIA:

I don't think the true form of Alpha, El Miore or El Cantare has been fully described. This is because human beings on earth can only still fathom things as three-dimensional existences with a height, width, and length; and they try to understand things along a timeline that is measurable with a clock.

If you asked me what the original form of Alpha was like, then I would describe him as having a ball in each hand. [*Gestures as if throwing a ball back and forth with each hand*]. One ball [*in right hand*] would represent space and the other [*in left hand*], time. Alpha could be described as being like a juggler who juggles time and space.

Do not try to define the universe through the eyes of time and space; in other words, do not try to determine the universe through the flow of time or through how space seems to be. Time and space are like balls that exist within the core essence of Alpha. It is the complete opposite of your perspective.

7

The Work of Creation on Earth

The most difficult thing
Was creating Earth's concept

SHIO OKAWA:

I imagine that there must have been various difficulties when Alpha was on earth giving guidance to people. Could you tell us what the biggest difficulty was?

GAIA:

Well, it was a period when an increasing number of living creatures were emerging from the sea to live on land. It was quite a challenge to make these aquatic species adjust to life on land. Creatures that were originally living in the ocean were beginning to adapt to terrestrial life. Among these terrestrial species, a few highly developed species began to emerge. It was a tremendous challenge to think of a way to give them a soul-like thing.

Furthermore, we had to differentiate what kind of traits should be "engraved" into each species. Some were given qualities similar to those that came from outer space, while others were given qualities unique to Earth. Basically, living creatures were being created as an experiment to test every conceivable possibility.

It began with the creation of the food chain system, so to speak, and from there began the introduction of human life. It was a challenge to make the Earth-born living creatures into the first ancestors of humankind.

Although human life forms were still in their experimental stages, there were various species from other planets that had crossed over the boundaries of time and space and tried to break into Earth through these "access holes."

It was difficult deciding whether we should allow them to live on Earth or not. However, the most difficult issue was creating the main objective for all life on Earth. In other words, it was the guiding concept of Earth.

In the past, an encyclopedic number of civilization experiments took place on different stars, star clusters and galaxies. Within the numerous possibilities, the most essential part of creation was to create a guiding concept for Earth's civilization. This means making the decision as to what the fundamentals of the terrestrial civilization would be. Making these decisions was the most difficult part of the process.

We created not only the terrestrial world, But Earth's Spirit World as well

GAIA:

So, it is hard for us to say whether time exists or not. It feels like I have been with Alpha for 600 million years, but it might have been only 300 million years ago when various things actually started to come into existence.

I am not sure what we were doing for the other 300 million years. I also can't tell if things back then happened in the physical world or the Spirit World. There probably was a planet called Earth, and I think it was enveloped by some kind of gaseous cloud of energy. There was also the job of turning this gaseous cloud of energy into the Spirit World.

In short, even the creation of the Earth's Spirit World was a job that needed to be done. It was not only the things on the surface of the Earth that had to be made; Earth's Spirit World also had to be created. So there were long periods of time when I could not determine whether we were in a spirit form or a physical form. Perhaps we could freely cross over between both worlds. I have a feeling that, unlike now, we were existences that could appear both in the Spirit World and the physical world.

In any case, the work of creation was quite difficult. It was a multifaceted task, and as such demanded a lot of care and attention.

I helped Alpha materialize His creations As His "right hand"

SHIO OKAWA:

You spoke of the creation of the Earth's Spirit World. Does the creation of the Spirit World mean the creation of order on Earth?

GAIA:

Yes. It means to decide the value system of this world. We must define which values are high and which are low. If the value system is different on another planet, then a completely different Spirit World would be created. For this system of the Earth, we must decide what makes the values higher or lower. This order must be linked to the way of living on this earth. This process was quite difficult to carry out.

SHIO OKAWA:

So Alpha devised such order, and your job was to help him?

GAIA:

Yes. If you ask me if I were an independent being, I might have been so. However, I am also aware that I was Alpha's "right hand," so I believe I helped embody His creations.

8

The Guiding Concept of Earth

The plan was to increase the evolution rate Compared to the Venusian civilization

SHIO OKAWA:

You mentioned that the most difficult task was deciding the guiding concept of Earth. Could you tell us what that concept was and also where the objective of this planet lies?

GAIA:

Different planets and star clusters have different objectives, and the degree of evolution between them varies quite considerably. When you create something new, you always need a concept.

In fact, the Venusian civilization existed prior to the Earth civilization. Alpha wanted to create something different while referring to the Venusian civilization as a basis.

I would say that harmony was a fairly strong quality of the civilization on Venus. Art and beauty certainly flourished in the long harmony that reigned, but at the same time, in some ways, the civilization on Venus stagnated and declined.

So, there was the original plan to increase the rate of evolution on Earth. Alpha introduced both a new system of creation and destruction as well as one of transition, and thought to create an environment that would give souls more opportunities to challenge themselves by making Earth a planet with relatively rapid changes.

The grand experiment on civilization: Harmonizing while evolving

GAIA:

In the early stages of the process, when there was a profusion of carnivorous species, there was a period when the survival of the fittest reigned. From the Venusian perspective, this was not necessarily a thing of beauty.

However, in fact, there were planets in the universe where the strong and the weak were fixed in their positions, and the weak were unilaterally enslaved by the strong. There were even some planets where the weak were captured as bait or food.

Still, Alpha's idea was to allow this power structure to exist, even if it appeared to be primitive, so that this structure would apply to today's market principle, or the principle of competition. His intention was for it to lead to the principle of human evolution through friendly competition.

So it was an experiment to give them the light of harmony while having them create a stir of competitiveness with one another to make progress. They then tried to strike a balance between harmony and progress. Their challenge was to balance these two aspects while creating a utopian world on Earth, and ultimately prevent that from falling apart.

The aim was not to continue a paradise without progress for billions of years. It was a big experiment on Earth civilization to create a world that continued to develop and evolve while still maintaining harmony.

A civilization that includes a mix of Pleiades, Vega, Venus and Magellanic influences

SHIO OKAWA:

There are a countless number of stars and planets in this universe. Is the concept of Earth original and unique to this planet?

GAIA:

There are no planets that are exactly same. Indeed, every star or planet differs slightly from another, so no two stars are exactly alike. For example, the characteristics of Venus are quite similar to those of the Pleiades[*], but also includes those of Vega[†] in some ways.

---

[*] The Pleiadians have an appearance that is very similar to the people on Earth. Their philosophy centers around love, beauty and harmony, as well as development. A lot of Pleiadians here on Earth are very supportive of the El Cantare spirit group. They are planning for a mass migration to Earth 1,000 years from now. Refer to Chapter 1 in *Breaking the Silence: Interviews with Space People* (Tokyo: Happy Science, 2013), Chapter 6 in *Uchu kara no Message* [Messages from the Universe] (Tokyo: IRH Press, 2011), and Chapter 1 in *Chikyu Wo Mamoru Uchu Rengo towa Nanika* [What is the Space Union that Protects Earth?] (Tokyo: IRH Press, 2011).

[†] Vega people, whose home planet is Vega in the constellation Lyra, have the ability to change their appearance to suit their own thoughts. The teachings of Vega mainly consist of moderation and harmony, as well as change. They have come to Earth with the objective to learn the laws of the Beginning and the laws of Origin from El Cantare. Refer to Chapter 4 in *Breaking the Silence: Interviews with Space People* (Tokyo: Happy Science, 2013), Chapters 3 and 4 in *Uchu kara no Shisha* [Messengers from the Universe] (Tokyo: IRH Press, 2011), and Chapter 1 in *Chikyu Wo Mamoru Uchu Rengo towa Nanika* [What is the Space Union that Protects Earth?] (Tokyo: IRH Press, 2011).

However, although the way of Earth is heavily influenced by the Pleiades and Vega, this does not mean that people on Earth can transform their appearance in the way the Vegans do. [In the case of Earth] Individuals are fixed to a certain degree. The civilization on Earth is influenced by stars such as the ones in the Pleiades, Vega and Venus, and also stars which have more violent characteristics. Aggressive stars, such as those of the Magellanic Clouds*, have also left a trace on Earth's culture.

I think Alpha was trying to mix and blend all different types of characteristics and create an entirely new civilization on Earth.

---

* In the Magellanic Clouds, there are numerous planets inhabited by very aggressive Reptilians [Reptile-like space people]. Their main planet is called Zeta. Earth accepted immigrants from the Magellanic Clouds over 300 million years ago. Refer to Chapter 3 in *Breaking the Silence: Interviews with Space People* (Tokyo: Happy Science, 2013), Chapter 1 in *Reptilian no Gyakushu I* [Reptilians Strike Back 1] (Tokyo: IRH Press, 2011), Chapter 1 in *The Laws of the Sun* (New York: IRH Press, 2018), and *The Laws of Alpha* (Tokyo: Happy Science, 2014).

9

The Meaning of El Cantare's Descent

Human beings have lost faith in their Creator And are starting to act like gods

SHIO OKAWA:

We are taught that Alpha was the first incarnation of the Fundamental Buddha on Earth. The second time He descended as Elohim. Today, He has descended for the third time as Master Ryuho Okawa. Could you explain what it means for the Fundamental Buddha to descend to earth?

We tend to think of Lord El Cantare as an extension of His branch spirits, such as Hermes or Shakyamuni Buddha. Please tell us why the Fundamental Buddha descended to earth now and what the similarities and differences are between Alpha's time and now.

GAIA:

The Earth civilization is being built up mainly by human beings. While there are differences among ethnic groups, humankind has been established as one group. The same thing is true for the animal kingdom. While some mutations and cross-breeding occur from time to time, the various species have by now almost all settled in their respective categories.

Moreover, compared to the time when humans were first created, they have evolved greatly, especially as individuals. While they have become increasingly admirable, they have become ever more oblivious to many important matters.

In the past, there was not as much distance communicating between the Spirit World and the material world. People fully understood the existence of the true world called the Spirit World and the fact that they are born on Earth, in a physical body, for soul training.

For example, in this world, you need food since you have a physical body. Thus, you must take the lives of other life forms in order to eat and survive. However, this situation never occurs in the Spirit World. In the past, people understood that the ways of the physical world are just temporary means for spiritual training. But as humans started to place more value on their lives in this world, they started to develop much stronger egos and identified themselves with their physical bodies. This is the big issue.

Comprehensively speaking, it could be said that human beings have lost faith in their Creator and that humans themselves are starting to act as though they are gods. Such a time is the modern era, I think.

The modern era is an extremely dangerous era Similar to the age of Elohim

GAIA:
There have been major issues in each era. The situation was grave in Elohim's time as well. In the age of Elohim, there were major space wars and a kind of nuclear war broke out on Earth. I think it was an extremely dangerous era for human beings.

During the age of Elohim, it was as clear as day that there were invaders coming to invade Earth, and they actually got involved in a war. Elohim seemingly made full use of His various abilities and also appeared as a type of warrior god.

Sometimes the god of creation and the god of destruction appeared in history. Back then was definitely an era when those who had no faith, meaning those who never listened to the voice of gods, were punished and annihilated.

In any case, it was a period when it was impossible to restrain the confusion created by space people and their human accomplices without weeding out those who had no faith and without establishing that faith.

Something very similar is happening in the modern age as well. Currently, there are a number of secret interventions by extraterrestrials, while observing and monitoring us humans. There is also in the air the possibility of a hegemonic war breaking out on Earth.

Atheism and materialism are infecting Earth like a malignant virus. Looking at this state with a spiritual eye from the universe, the current state of Earth is like "cheese covered with mold." The modern age holds a sense of crisis in that we must do something to remove the mold on the surface of the cheese.

The purpose is to begin
A spiritual revolution on a Global Level

SHIO OKAWA:

How much is Lord El Cantare actually aiming to accomplish by descending to Earth this time? It would be great if you could tell us as much as you know.

GAIA:

Modern people hardly listen [to the Voice of God]. Even Christians are gradually losing faith in God and there are so many atheists who claim to be Buddhists. Science has made great advancements in the past 200 to 300 years, but there are many scientists and doctors who do not believe in the existence of a soul or God.

People are losing sight of such matters by receiving modern education. The era that puts aside the issue of spirituality is coming. In this sense, there is no doubt that He is trying to start a spiritual revolution on a global level.

It is a revolution of spirituality.
It is also a revolution of the right path as a religion,
An attempt to have people admit
That humans are spiritual beings.
It is also an educational revolution.
It is also a political revolution.

I think that He is also trying to prevent the historical scenario of the evil countries, in the military aspect, from being accomplished, since the modern world holds the danger of evil countries trying to destroy the ones that are not.

It seems to me that, in the future, His eventual goal is to transform factors of totalitarianism held by Communists and Muslims. As He does so, He will probably change the nature of brutality in humans and try to make that energy flow in the direction of growth and advancement. In short, He will try to use that energy of lust not for creating conflicts on Earth but for friendly competition toward the space age.

Harmonizing the Earth civilization
Is a requisite for the space age

SHIO OKAWA:
As a being who was present in the time of Genesis, what do you think of the Earth today?

GAIA:
The population did grow significantly.

Although you cannot tell them apart with your physical eyes, as a matter of fact, there are a wide variety of souls that have taken form as humans. Among them, there are the souls from outer space and those which evolved from animal souls. It is not an easy task to distinguish between them because they have been treated and educated as humans through their physical DNA and culture.

There must be some sense of happiness for such souls to be born as humans, but we have to be very careful that their own personal happiness will not lead Earth to chaos and destruction. What is important at first is to teach them the truth.

I guess what I am talking about all sounds like stories from Mythology.

However, along with the advancement of science enabling us to travel into outer space, the population of Earth has increased to over seven billion and will soon surpass ten billion. It is only a matter of time before the human race will split and migrate to other planets.

With the approach of such era, purification and beautification and the great "cleanup" for disharmony of the Earth civilization would be required. I think that He strongly feels the need to harmonize the civilizations on Earth before they [Earth people] start leaving for outer space. I think He is trying to achieve this.

It is only a matter of time until Happy Science becomes the religion of Earth

GAIA:

All of you who live in the same era as El Cantare probably think that Happy Science only makes up a small portion of the recent world religions. However, it is only a matter of time before Happy Science encompasses the whole world as a big religion.

Those with wisdom, listen to me.
You shall see the depth,
The level and the expanse of these teachings,
And must understand
That Happy Science is the religion of Earth.
You must understand
That this teaching is destined
To encompass the Earth and even the universe
In the light of both time and space.
Until that time comes,
You have been given
The challenge to endeavor and persevere
As humans.

The new crisis of annihilation
That Earth people are now facing

GAIA:

What humans believe to be "prosperity" is something different from what God desires. And this will give rise to a new crisis of annihilation.

The wrong part of "prosperity" is actually causing evil to spread on earth. When the level of evil surpasses a certain amount, from the perspective of belligerent alien species, Earth would appear like a safari park with the permission to hunt. On a cosmic scale, this situation could allow alien species to be granted a permission to hunt or destroy around 10 billion evil Earth people. In order to prevent this from happening, El Cantare is proceeding with the purification process.

10

The Truth Behind
The Name "Gaia"

SHIO OKAWA:

Excuse me for changing the subject a little, but in Greek mythology, Gaia is referred to as the goddess of earth. Could you tell me if the name *Gaia* has a meaning?

GAIA:

I have used the name *Gaia* in order to make it easy to understand for people today. The word *Gaia* means "Earth" or "Mother Earth." It means what it means.

However, Alpha and I were not given the names *Alpha* and *Gaia* as humans are given names on earth.

Our names were not of such kind; we were who we were.

Whether you call this existence Alpha,
Or Light,
Or the Origin,

Or Heavenly Father,
Or Lord,
Or whatever else it may be,
Actually, it doesn't matter.
However,
If put in a modern way,
Alpha, the God of Origin
Would suit Him.

The same goes for Gaia.
Gaia was the catalyst
When Alpha worked
To create the world.
Gaia's role
Was to assist and enhance
Alpha's work of creation.
Therefore,
Gaia is "the one who nurtures"
And "the one who protects life."

In this sense, the role of Gaia is equivalent to the name
Gaia. You may assume that the name is being used to
make it easier to understand for modern people.

I mentioned earlier that I was the hand [of El Cantare], so you can even call me "God's hand," but I feel that the name Gaia would be easier to understand for the people of this age. That is why I call myself so.

11

Boundless Adoration
For the Parent of Our Souls

SHIO OKAWA:

We were given the title, "In Love with the Sun" this time. What kind of an existence is the Sun to you, and what kind of thoughts and messages are put into the title?

GAIA:

That would be the ultimate source of Alpha.

What is the ultimate source?
It is the source of all life.
The sunlight is the source of all life on Earth.
The sun is what nurtures all life.
This is at least true
In the three-dimensional realm.
At the same time,
There is a power at work,
In the Spirit World,
That nurtures all spiritual beings.

The massive power of the sun
In the Spirit World
Actually gives life
And nurtures all living beings on Earth
And allows them to grow and thrive.
This is the essence of Alpha.
What corresponds to the sun
In the Spirit World
Is actually the essence of Alpha.

Of course,
There exists a consciousness and purpose
In its depth,
Which go far beyond the Sun
In our Solar System.
However, the question is,
Who is the real God of Earth
As the God of Origin.
There are many deities that appear in the myths
Of various countries and ethnic groups.
But if we were to confirm the God of Origin
Beyond all myths in each of them,
Alpha is the One
Who stands above all.

This is what I am trying to say.
The title, "In Love with the Sun"
Expresses my boundless adoration and longing
For the parent of our souls.
Many countries such as Japan and Egypt
Have religions that worship the sun.
In the depths of sun worship,
Are feelings of reverence toward the power of all life.
It is a sense of belief
Toward the power of creation and making.
It is the Beginning
Or the Original Thought
Or the starting point of all things.
It is the ultimate question in philosophy:
What is the origin of all things?
The being at the starting point of all questions
Is Alpha.
In other words,
You can see the beginning of Earth,
The development of Earth
And what was there before Earth appeared,
Through Alpha.

I, Gaia,

Have always been with Alpha.

And as much as I was the one who assisted His work,

I feel I am always one with Him

Through something like deep love toward Him,

Similar to worshipping the sun.

SHIO OKAWA:

Thank you very much.

12

A Spiritual Revolution Will Occur Within the Next 10 Years

SHIO OKAWA:

This will be my last question.

The Lord has taught us that He will show His true form only when the disciples are ready. We, disciples, were given life in the same era as Lord El Cantare and have witnessed the kind of work the Fundamental Buddha carries out. We have all gathered to the Lord and have been given the positions to support Him. Is there anything that we, disciples, should keep in mind as we follow the Lord?

GAIA:

Actually, the work has been proceeding beneath the surface much more than you think. Since Japanese people have the tendency of not mentioning or explaining everything, it's hard to tell. In fact, however, things that Happy Science has created are gradually prevailing in the entire culture that is being developed by Japanese people.

For example, although a new administration is about to take power in Japan, at the center of its political ideas are almost everything that were created and released by Happy Science.

In other words, it is like March
When spring is just around the corner.
The thick ice on the lake is thinning,
And is about to crack and melt away.
But until the thin ice completely melts away,
You continue to think
That the world beneath the ice
And the world above the ice
Are completely separated by this thick wall.
The truth of the matter is,
The warm spring breeze
Is gradually melting away the ice,
Little by little.

You all may think we are far from reaching the goal.
However,
A great start to a mental revolution,
A spirituality revolution,
Or a spiritual revolution,

Has been approaching.
It shall surely happen
Within the next 10 years.
This spiritual revolution shall open the next stage.
I believe so.

The most crucial focus at this point is to build up the country of Japan as the country of God, but at the same time, you should plant seeds of Truth in other countries around the world.

Although there may be a time lag between the two processes, the teachings of Happy Science must have attained the status of a national religion or have become a national polity by the time the flowers of the seeds planted in other nations start to bloom.

Such must be the final form of our faith.
If the God of Origin
Begins His work as the God of Origin,
Such a form shall be realized.

It is impossible
For His work to end

At the same level
As Jesus Christ
Or Shakyamuni Buddha.
His work will reach the level
To where the world will recognize
The importance of His existence
While He is alive.
His disciples will achieve
A hundred times,
A thousand times,
Or ten thousand times greater work
Than they are aware of at the moment.
I believe so.

SHIO OKAWA:
We will make great efforts in order to make all of that come true. Thank you very much for your time today.

GAIA:
OK.

RYUHO OKAWA:
[*To Gaia.*] Thank you very much.

13

Aim to Become
A Global Scale Religion

RYUHO OKAWA:

I wonder if this was good enough. I wonder if we should have asked someone else. I feel that the existence of Gaia has now become even more vague. It's completely behind the clouds.

While the title of this spiritual message, "In Love with the Sun," sounds a bit unusual, what comes out in the beginning of a year generally prophesizes what will happen in that year to some extent.

Last year [2012], I conducted, "Nichigin Sosai to no Spiritual Taiwa" [Spiritual Conversation with the Governor of the Bank of Japan], and the content of the conversation was actually implemented in the government the following year.*

---

* Refer to *Nichigin Sosai to no Spiritual Taiwa* [Spiritual Conversation with the Governor of the Bank of Japan] (Tokyo: IRH Press, 2012).

Hence, the fact that the spiritual messages from Gaia, titled "In Love with the Sun," were recorded means that a year from now, the world must be closer to the state described in the messages.

You must remember what Gaia just said and must think that the ice on the lake is starting to thin. Although you still cannot see that the ice is thinning because you are on the shore, you must know that this ice will melt away when spring comes. You all may consider the ice as the wall or an obstacle to our progression, but in reality the ice has melted enough to the point where you can see through the ice and to the bottom of the lake.

The important content in today's messages is to not neglect the process of preparing for the day when the ice has completely melted away.

It is fine to think that this appearance of a new 'Genesis' is the declaration of a global scale religion beginning its activities. It also would be safe to believe that our confidence is growing toward it.

There is much more to be said and preached if we include the teachings on the universe." Much, much deeper and hidden teachings will be revealed in accordance with our maturity, awareness and acceptance.

Gaia said that a spiritual revolution will occur within the next 10 years, so each of you must keep making efforts. By a year from now, we will probably see more of what was said in the messages happening.

Let us devote ourselves in preparation for that day.

Thank you very much.

Afterword

Now that you have finished reading this book, what are your thoughts?

The most important message we wanted to deliver to you through this book was that the Creator existed long, long time ago and that all life, including humankind, was created by Him.

We can say that each and every one of us is precious simply because we are an existence created by that God. The ethical values taught to us in schools that "the life of each and every one of us is precious without exception" comes from this truth. No matter how much you call for the dignity of life or other ethical values, without acknowledging this truth, your words will only sound shallow. You can only be called a yeller who does not know the real meaning of the dignity of life.

I believe this book will bring about a significant change in the concept of Genesis. The book will also confront, face-to-face, materialistic thoughts that ridicule God and that defies invisible things or spiritual values.

But the truth is the truth. I sincerely hope that this truth will reach as many people as possible.

"The Sun" has re-revealed itself to us and is preaching the Truth; this, too, is a truth.

From the very beginning until this very moment, the God of Origin has always been pouring His love for us. It would bring me great joy if you could feel even a slight bit of the love from the God of Origin through this book.

Finally, I would like to express my heartfelt thanks for this opportunity.

Shio Okawa
Aide to Master & CEO

ABOUT THE AUTHORS

Founder and CEO of Happy Science Group

Ryuho Okawa

Ryuho Okawa was born on July 7th 1956, in Tokushima, Japan. After graduating from the University of Tokyo with a law degree, he joined a Tokyo-based trading house. While working at its New York headquarters, he studied international finance at the Graduate Center of the City University of New York. In 1981, he attained Great Enlightenment and became aware that he is El Cantare with a mission to bring salvation to all humankind.

In 1986, he established Happy Science. It now has members in over 165 countries across the world, with more than 700 branches and temples as well as 10,000 missionary houses around the world.

He has given over 3,450 lectures (of which more than 150 are in English) and published over 3,000 books (of which more than 600 are Spiritual Interview Series), and many are translated into 40 languages. Along with *The Laws of the Sun* and *The Laws Of Messiah*, many of the books have become best sellers or million sellers. To date, Happy Science has produced 25 movies. The original story and original concept were given by the Executive Producer Ryuho Okawa. He has also composed music and written lyrics of over 450 pieces.

Moreover, he is the Founder of Happy Science University and Happy Science Academy (Junior and Senior High School), Founder and President of the Happiness Realization Party, Founder and Honorary Headmaster of Happy Science Institute of Government and Management, Founder of IRH Press Co., Ltd., and the Chairperson of NEW STAR PRODUCTION Co., Ltd. and ARI Production Co., Ltd.

Aide to Master & CEO
Shio Okawa

Shio Okawa is the Aide to Master & CEO and is the wife of Master Ryuho Okawa. Born in 1985 in Tokushima, Japan. Shio graduated from the Faculty of Law at Waseda University, then worked at the Bank of Japan before joining Happy Science as a staff member in 2009. At Happy Science, she assumed positions such as Chief Secretary of First Secretarial Division in Religious Affairs Headquarters and Senior Managing Director. She has written books and picture books such as "Introduction to the 'Panda Method'," "Aiming to become a Competent Woman," "Transformation to Panguru," the Panda Roonda picture book series, "Panda's Transformation," "Llama and King Lyga," "Angulimala – A Story of Sin and Forgiveness," and "The Song of Spring." Shio also wrote *In Love with the Sun* in collaboration with Master Ryuho Okawa and "Make a Great Country, Japan!" with Ryoko Shaku, the Party Leader of the Happiness Realization Party. Shio also created the concept for the film, *The Divine Protector – Master Salt Begins*. In addition, she wrote the lyrics of a mini-album, "The Songs of Spring, Summer, Autumn, and Winter" (all titles in double quotation are tentative translations).

WHAT IS EL CANTARE?

El Cantare means "the Light of the Earth," and is the Supreme God of the Earth who has been guiding humankind since the beginning of Genesis. He is whom Jesus called Father and Muhammad called Allah, and is *Ame-no-Mioya-Gami*, Japanese Father God. Different parts of El Cantare's core consciousness have descended to Earth in the past, once as Alpha and another as Elohim. His branch spirits, such as Shakyamuni Buddha and Hermes, have descended to Earth many times and helped to flourish many civilizations. To unite various religions and to integrate various fields of study in order to build a new civilization on Earth, a part of the core consciousness has descended to Earth as Master Ryuho Okawa.

Alpha is a part of the core consciousness of El Cantare who descended to Earth around 330 million years ago. Alpha preached Earth's Truths to harmonize and unify Earth-born humans and space people who came from other planets.

Elohim is a part of El Cantare's core consciousness who descended to Earth around 150 million years ago. He gave wisdom, mainly on the differences of light and darkness, good and evil.

Ame-no-Mioya-Gami (Japanese Father God) is the Creator God and the Father God who appears in the ancient literature, *Hotsuma Tsutae*. It is believed that He descended on the foothills of Mt. Fuji about 30,000 years ago and built the Fuji dynasty, which is the root of the Japanese civilization. With justice as the central pillar, Ame-no-Mioya-Gami's teachings spread to ancient civilizations of other countries in the world.

Shakyamuni Buddha was born as a prince into the Shakya Clan in India around 2,600 years ago. When he was 29 years old, he renounced the world and sought enlightenment. He later attained Great Enlightenment and founded Buddhism.

Hermes is one of the 12 Olympian gods in Greek mythology, but the spiritual Truth is that he taught the teachings of love and progress around 4,300 years ago that became the origin of the current Western civilization. He is a hero that truly existed.

Ophealis was born in Greece around 6,500 years ago and was the leader who took an expedition to as far as Egypt. He is the God of miracles, prosperity, and arts, and is known as Osiris in the Egyptian mythology.

Rient Arl Croud was born as a king of the ancient Incan Empire around 7,000 years ago and taught about the mysteries of the mind. In the heavenly world, he is responsible for the interactions that take place between various planets.

Thoth was an almighty leader who built the golden age of the Atlantic civilization around 12,000 years ago. In the Egyptian mythology, he is known as god Thoth.

Ra Mu was a leader who built the golden age of the civilization of Mu around 17,000 years ago. As a religious leader and a politician, he ruled by uniting religion and politics.

WHAT IS A SPIRITUAL MESSAGE?

We are all spiritual beings living on this earth. The following is the mechanism behind Master Ryuho Okawa's spiritual messages.

1 You are a spirit

People are born into this world to gain wisdom through various experiences and return to the other world when their lives end. We are all spirits and repeat this cycle in order to refine our souls.

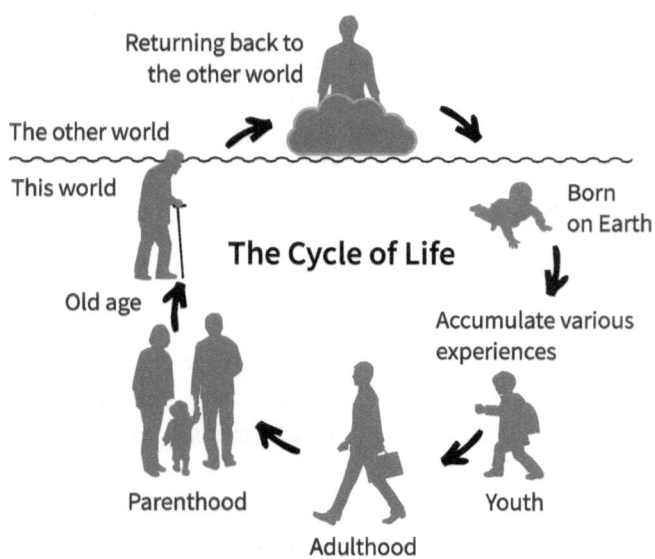

Returning back to the other world

The other world

This world

Born on Earth

The Cycle of Life

Old age

Accumulate various experiences

Parenthood

Adulthood

Youth

2 You have a guardian spirit

Guardian spirits are those who protect the people who are living on this earth. Each of us has a guardian spirit that watches over us and guides us from the other world. They were us in our past life, and are identical in how we think.

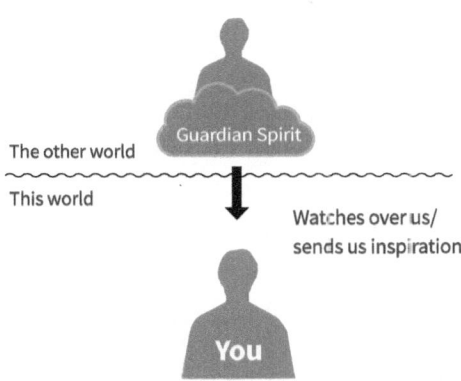

3 How spiritual messages work

Master Ryuho Okawa, through his enlightenment, is capable of summoning any spirit from anywhere in the world, including the spirit world.

Master Okawa's way of receiving spiritual messages is fundamentally different from that of other psychic mediums who undergo trances and are thereby completely taken over by the spirits they are channeling.

Master Okawa's attainment of a high level of enlightenment enables him to retain full control of his consciousness and body throughout the duration of the spiritual message. To allow the spirits to express their own thoughts and personalities freely, however, Master Okawa usually softens the dominancy of his consciousness. This way, he is able to keep his own philosophies out of the way and ensure that the spiritual messages are pure expressions of the spirits he is channeling.

Since guardian spirits think at the same subconscious level as the person living on earth, Master Okawa can summon the spirit and find out what the person on earth is actually thinking. If the person has already returned to the other world, the spirit can give messages to the people living on earth through Master Okawa.

Since 2009, many spiritual messages have been openly recorded by Master Okawa and published. Spiritual messages from the guardian spirits of people living today such as Donald Trump, former Japanese Prime Minister Shinzo Abe and Chinese President Xi Jinping, as well as spiritual messages sent from the spirit world by Jesus Christ, Muhammad, Thomas Edison, Mother Teresa, Steve Jobs and Nelson Mandela are just a tiny pack of spiritual messages that were published so far.

Domestically, in Japan, these spiritual messages are being read by a wide range of politicians and mass media, and the high-level contents of these books are delivering an impact even more on politics, news and public opinion. In recent years, there have been spiritual messages recorded in English, and

English translations are being done on the spiritual messages given in Japanese. These have been published overseas, one after another, and have started to shake the world.

1 The guardian spirit / spirit in the other world...

2 Goes inside Master Okawa in this world

3 Master Okawa speaks the words of the guardian spirit / spirit

For more about spiritual messages and a complete list of books in the Spiritual Interview Series, visit okawabooks.com

ABOUT HAPPY SCIENCE

Happy Science is a global movement that empowers individuals to find purpose and spiritual happiness and to share that happiness with their families, societies, and the world. With more than 12 million members around the world, Happy Science aims to increase awareness of spiritual truths and expand our capacity for love, compassion, and joy so that together we can create the kind of world we all wish to live in.

Activities at Happy Science are based on the Principle of Happiness (Love, Wisdom, Self-Reflection, and Progress). This principle embraces worldwide philosophies and beliefs, transcending boundaries of culture and religions.

Love teaches us to give ourselves freely without expecting anything in return; it encompasses giving, nurturing, and forgiving.

Wisdom leads us to the insights of spiritual truths, and opens us to the true meaning of life and the will of God (the universe, the highest power, Buddha).

Self-Reflection brings a mindful, nonjudgmental lens to our thoughts and actions to help us find our truest selves—the essence of our souls—and deepen our connection to the highest power. It helps us attain a clean and peaceful mind and leads us to the right life path.

Progress emphasizes the positive, dynamic aspects of our spiritual growth—actions we can take to manifest and spread happiness around the world. It's a path that not only expands our soul growth, but also furthers the collective potential of the world we live in.

PROGRAMS AND EVENTS

The doors of Happy Science are open to all. We offer a variety of programs and events, including self-exploration and self-growth programs, spiritual seminars, meditation and contemplation sessions, study groups, and book events.

Our programs are designed to:
* Deepen your understanding of your purpose and meaning in life
* Improve your relationships and increase your capacity to love unconditionally
* Attain peace of mind, decrease anxiety and stress, and feel positive
* Gain deeper insights and a broader perspective on the world
* Learn how to overcome life's challenges
    ... and much more.

For more information, visit <u>happy-science.org</u>.

OUR ACTIVITIES

Happy Science does other various activities to provide support for those in need.

◆ **You Are An Angel! General Incorporated Association**
Happy Science has a volunteer network in Japan that encourages and supports children with disabilities as well as their parents and guardians.

◆ **Never Mind School for Truancy**
At 'Never Mind,' we support students who find it very challenging to attend schools in Japan. We also nurture their self-help spirit and power to rebound against obstacles in life based on Master Okawa's teachings and faith.

◆ **"Prevention Against Suicide" Campaign since 2003**
A nationwide campaign to reduce suicides; over 20,000 people commit suicide every year in Japan. "The Suicide Prevention Website-Words of Truth for You-" presents spiritual prescriptions for worries such as depression, lost love, extramarital affairs, bullying and work-related problems, thereby saving many lives.

◆ **Support for Anti-bullying Campaigns**
Happy Science provides support for a group of parents and guardians, Network to Protect Children from Bullying, a general incorporated foundation launched in Japan to end bullying, including those that can even be called a criminal offense. So far, the network received more than 5,000 cases and resolved 90% of them.

♦ **The Golden Age Scholarship**

This scholarship is granted to students who can contribute greatly and bring a hopeful future to the world.

♦ **Success No.1**
Buddha's Truth Afterschool Academy

Happy Science has over 180 classrooms throughout Japan and in several cities around the world that focus on afterschool education for children. The education focuses on faith and morals in addition to supporting children's school studies.

♦ **Angel Plan V**

For children under the age of kindergarten, Happy Science holds classes for nurturing healthy, positive, and creative boys and girls.

♦ **Future Stars Training Department**

The Future Stars Training Department was founded within the Happy Science Media Division with the goal of nurturing talented individuals to become successful in the performing arts and entertainment industry.

♦ **NEW STAR PRODUCTION Co., Ltd.**
ARI Production Co., Ltd.

We have companies to nurture actors and actresses, artists, and vocalists. They are also involved in film production.

CONTACT INFORMATION

Happy Science is a worldwide organization with branches and temples around the globe. For a comprehensive list, visit the worldwide directory at *happy-science.org*. The following are some of the many Happy Science locations:

UNITED STATES AND CANADA

New York
79 Franklin St., New York, NY 10013, USA
Phone: 1-212-343-7972
Fax: 1-212-343-7973
Email: ny@happy-science.org
Website: happyscience-usa.org

New Jersey
66 Hudson St., #2R, Hoboken, NJ 07030, USA
Phone: 1-201-313-0127
Email: nj@happy-science.org
Website: happyscience-usa.org

Chicago
2300 Barrington Rd., Suite #400,
Hoffman Estates, IL 60169, USA
Phone: 1-630-937-3077
Email: chicago@happy-science.org
Website: happyscience-usa.org

Florida
5208 8th St., Zephyrhills, FL 33542, USA
Phone: 1-813-715-0000
Fax: 1-813-715-0010
Email: florida@happy-science.org
Website: happyscience-usa.org

Atlanta
1874 Piedmont Ave., NE Suite 360-C
Atlanta, GA 30324, USA
Phone: 1-404-892-7770
Email: atlanta@happy-science.org
Website: happyscience-usa.org

San Francisco
525 Clinton St.
Redwood City, CA 94062, USA
Phone & Fax: 1-650-363-2777
Email: sf@happy-science.org
Website: happyscience-usa.org

Los Angeles
1590 E. Del Mar Blvd., Pasadena, CA 91106, USA
Phone: 1-626-395-7775
Fax: 1-626-395-7776
Email: la@happy-science.org
Website: happyscience-usa.org

Orange County
16541 Gothard St. Suite 104
Huntington Beach, CA 92647
Phone: 1-714-659-1501
Email: oc@happy-science.org
Website: happyscience-usa.org

San Diego
7841 Balboa Ave. Suite #202
San Diego, CA 92111, USA
Phone: 1-626-395-7775
Fax: 1-626-395-7776
E-mail: sandiego@happy-science.org
Website: happyscience-usa.org

Hawaii
Phone: 1-808-591-9772
Fax: 1-808-591-9776
Email: hi@happy-science.org
Website: happyscience-usa.org

Kauai
3343 Kanakolu Street, Suite 5
Lihue, HI 96766, USA
Phone: 1-808-822-7007
Fax: 1-808-822-6007
Email: kauai-hi@happy-science.org
Website: happyscience-usa.org

Toronto
845 The Queensway
Etobicoke, ON M8Z 1N6, Canada
Phone: 1-416-901-3747
Email: toronto@happy-science.org
Website: happy-science.ca

Vancouver
#201-2607 East 49th Avenue,
Vancouver, BC, V5S 1J9, Canada
Phone: 1-604-437-7735
Fax: 1-604-437-7764
Email: vancouver@happy-science.org
Website: happy-science.ca

INTERNATIONAL

Tokyo
1-6-7 Togoshi, Shinagawa,
Tokyo, 142-0041, Japan
Phone: 81-3-6384-5770
Fax: 81-3-6384-5776
Email: tokyo@happy-science.org
Website: happy-science.org

Seoul
74, Sadang-ro 27-gil,
Dongjak-gu, Seoul, Korea
Phone: 82-2-3478-8777
Fax: 82-2-3478-9777
Email: korea@happy-science.org
Website: happyscience-korea.org

London
3 Margaret St.
London, W1W 8RE United Kingdom
Phone: 44-20-7323-9255
Fax: 44-20-7323-9344
Email: eu@happy-science.org
Website: www.happyscience-uk.org

Taipei
No. 89, Lane 155, Dunhua N. Road,
Songshan District, Taipei City 105, Taiwan
Phone: 886-2-2719-9377
Fax: 886-2-2719-5570
Email: taiwan@happy-science.org
Website: happyscience-tw.org

Sydney
516 Pacific Highway, Lane Cove North,
2066 NSW, Australia
Phone: 61-2-9411-2877
Fax: 61-2-9411-2822
Email: sydney@happy-science.org

Kuala Lumpur
No 22A, Block 2, Jalil Link Jalan Jalil
Jaya 2, Bukit Jalil 57000,
Kuala Lumpur, Malaysia
Phone: 60-3-8998-7877
Fax: 60-3-8998-7977
Email: malaysia@happy-science.org
Website: happyscience.org.my

Sao Paulo
Rua. Domingos de Morais 1154,
Vila Mariana, Sao Paulo SP
CEP 04010-100, Brazil
Phone: 55-11-5088-3800
Email: sp@happy-science.org
Website: happyscience.com.br

Kathmandu
Kathmandu Metropolitan City,
Ward No. 15, Ring Road, Kimdol,
Sitapaila Kathmandu, Nepal
Phone: 977-1-427-2931
Email: nepal@happy-science.org

Jundiai
Rua Congo, 447, Jd. Bonfiglioli
Jundiai-CEP, 13207-340, Brazil
Phone: 55-11-4587-5952
Email: jundiai@happy-science.org

Kampala
Plot 877 Rubaga Road, Kampala
P.O. Box 34130 Kampala, UGANDA
Phone: 256-79-4682-121
Email: uganda@happy-science.org

ABOUT HS PRESS

HS Press is an imprint of IRH Press Co., Ltd. IRH Press Co., Ltd., based in Tokyo, was founded in 1987 as a publishing division of Happy Science. IRH Press publishes religious and spiritual books, journals, magazines and also operates broadcast and film production enterprises. For more information, visit *okawabooks.com*.

Follow us on:

f Facebook: Okawa Books   Instagram: OkawaBooks
Youtube: Okawa Books   Twitter: Okawa Books
Pinterest: Okawa Books   Goodreads: Ryuho Okawa

——— **NEWSLETTER** ———

To receive book related news, promotions and events, please subscribe to our newsletter below.

eepurl.com/bsMeJj

 ——— **AUDIO / VISUAL MEDIA** ———

YOUTUBE

PODCAST

Introduction of Ryuho Okawa's titles; topics ranging from self-help, current affairs, spirituality, religion, and the universe.

BOOKS BY RYUHO OKAWA

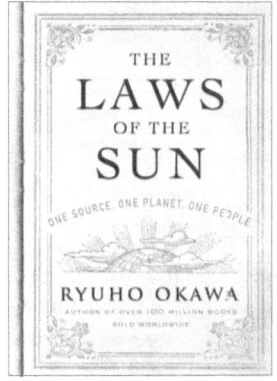

THE LAWS OF THE SUN

ONE SOURCE, ONE PLANET, ONE PEOPLE

Paperback • 288 pages • $15.95
ISBN: 978-1-942125-43-3

IMAGINE IF YOU COULD ASK GOD why He created this world and what spiritual laws He used to shape us—and everything around us. If we could understand His designs and intentions, we could discover what our goals in life should be and whether our actions move us closer to those goals or farther away.

At a young age, a spiritual calling prompted Ryuho Okawa to outline what he innately understood to be universal truths for all humankind. In *The Laws of the Sun*, Okawa outlines these laws of the universe and provides a road map for living one's life with greater purpose and meaning.

In this powerful book, Ryuho Okawa reveals the transcendent nature of consciousness and the secrets of our multidimensional universe and our place in it. By understanding the different stages of love and following the Buddhist Eightfold Path, he believes we can speed up our eternal process of development. *The Laws of the Sun* shows the way to realize true happiness—a happiness that continues from this world through the other.

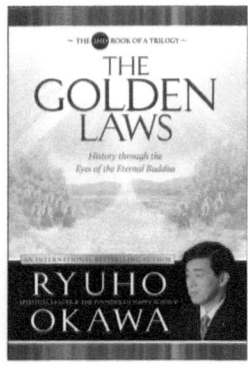

THE GOLDEN LAWS

HISTORY THROUGH THE EYES OF THE ETERNAL BUDDHA

Paperback • 201 pages • $14.95
ISBN: 978-1-941779-81-1

Throughout history, Great Guiding Spirits of Light have been present on Earth in both the East and the West at crucial points in human history to further our spiritual development. *The Golden Laws* reveals how Divine Plan has been unfolding on Earth, and outlines 5,000 years of the secret history of humankind. Once we understand the true course of history, through past, present and into the future, we cannot help but become aware of the significance of our spiritual mission in the present age.

THE NINE DIMENSIONS

UNVEILING THE LAWS OF ETERNITY

Paperback • 168 pages • $15.95
ISBN: 978-0-982698-56-3

This book is a window into the mind of our loving God, who designed this world and the vast, wondrous world of our afterlife as a school with many levels through which our souls learn and grow. When the religions and cultures of the world discover the truth of their common spiritual origin, they will be inspired to accept their differences, come together under faith in God, and build an era of harmony and peaceful progress on Earth.

SECRETS OF THE EVERLASTING TRUTHS

A NEW PARADIGM FOR LIVING ON EARTH

Paperback • 142 pages • $14.95
ISBN: 978-1-937673-10-9

OUR BELIEF IN THE INVISIBLE IS OUR FUTURE. It is our knowledge about the everlasting spiritual laws and our belief in the invisible that will make it possible for us to solve the world's problems and bring our entire planet together. When you discover the secrets in this book, your view of yourself and the world will be changed dramatically and forever.

THE LAWS OF PERSEVERANCE

REVERSING YOUR COMMON SENSE

Paperback • 268 pages • $14.95
ISBN: 978-1-937673-56-7

"No matter how much you suffer, the Truth will gradually shine forth as you continue to endure hardships. Therefore, simply strengthen your mind and keep making constant efforts in times of endurance, however ordinary they may be. "

-From Postscript

THINK BIG!

BE POSITIVE AND BE BRAVE TO ACHIEVE YOUR DREAMS!

ISBN: 978-1-941779-06-4

$14.95 (Paperback)

In *Think Big* Master Ryuho Okawa shares his own philosophy of thinking big, thinking positive, and being brave for they are essential mindsets in achieving our dreams. While there is an especial emphasis on developing this philosophy while we're young, it is universal and valuable for people of all ages and all walks of life who want to achieve their dreams and live a successful life. If you do not have any dreams yet, then this is a must-have book for discovering why having ideals are an essential part of life. If you already have aspirations, then discover how to make them come true. If you are in college, find out valuable tips on how to get a head start on developing the think big mindset.

THE TEN PRINCIPLES FROM EL CANTARE
VOLUME I
Ryuho Okawa's First Lectures on His Basic Teachings

THE TEN PRINCIPLES FROM EL CANTARE
VOLUME II
Ryuho Okawa's First Lectures on His Wish to Save the World

THE STARTING POINT OF HAPPINESS
A Practical and Intuitive Guide to Discovering Love, Wisdom, and Faith

LOVE, NURTURE, AND FORGIVE
A Handbook to Add a New Richness to Your Life

AN UNSHAKABLE MIND
How to Overcome Life's Difficulties

THE ORIGIN OF LOVE
On the Beauty of Compassion

INVINCIBLE THINKING
An Essential Guide for a Lifetime of Growth, Success, and Triumph

GUIDEPOSTS TO HAPPINESS
Prescriptions for a Wonderful Life

THE LAWS OF HAPPINESS
Love, Wisdom, Self-Reflection and Progress

TIPS TO FIND HAPPINESS
Creating a Harmonious Home for Your Spouse,
Your Children, and Yourself

THE PHILOSOPHY OF PROGRESS
Higher Thinking for Developing Infinite Prosperity

THE ESSENCE OF BUDDHA
The Path to Enlightenment

THE CHALLENGE OF THE MIND
An Essential Guide to Buddha's Teachings: Zen, Karma, and Enlightenment

THE CHALLENGE OF ENLIGHTENMENT
Realize Your Inner Potential

THE MANIFESTO OF THE HAPPINESS
REALIZATION PARTY

RYUHO OKAWA: A POLITICAL REVOLUTIONARY
The Originator of Abenomics and Father of
the Happiness Realization Party

SPIRITUAL MESSAGES FROM
THE GUARDIAN SPIRIT OF RYUHO OKAWA
The Divine Voice of Shakyamuni Buddha

THE IMPORTANCE OF
THE EXPLORATION OF THE RIGHT MIND

HIGHER EDUCATION SERIES

THE NEW IDEA OF A UNIVERSITY
The Groundbreaking Mission of Happy Science University

THE BASIC TEACHINGS OF HAPPY SCIENCE
A Happiness Theory on Truth and Faith

THE TRUTH OF THE PACIFIC WAR

Soulful Messages from Hideki Tojo,
Japan's Wartime Leader

ISBN: 978-1-941779-22-4
$14.95 (Paperback)

In this book, we provide you with the material needed to rethink whether or not the perception of World War II by the winners was right, through looking back on history starting with the current world affairs. This is all necessary for us to get a thorough understanding of ongoing confusion in the world and to seek the path of peace, stability and progress of future humankind.

The material provided is a new testimony by General Hideki Tojo, who is enshrined at Yasukuni Shrine and who was Japan's most significant figure in the Pacific War. Furthermore, we have also recorded a testimony by Supreme Commander of the Allied Powers Douglas MacArthur in order to ensure a fair argument.

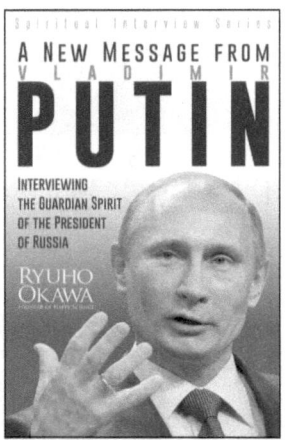

A NEW MESSAGE FROM
VLADIMIR PUTIN
Interviewing the Guardian Spirit of the President of Russia

ISBN: 978-1-937673-94-9
$14.95 (Paperback)

We hereby bring you the most recent spiritual message from the guardian spirit of President Putin, the politician who is the center of attention of not just the people of Russia but of the whole world, regardless of it being in a good or a bad way. In the Preface, it says, "President Putin's true intentions, which are 90 percent misunderstood."

We hope that, through this book, the reader will come to understand the true thoughts of Mr. Putin which are still undisclosed to the public. And, we hope that the reader will foresee the new world order that this skilled politician is thinking of, and make use of that in predicting how the international affairs will turn out in the future.

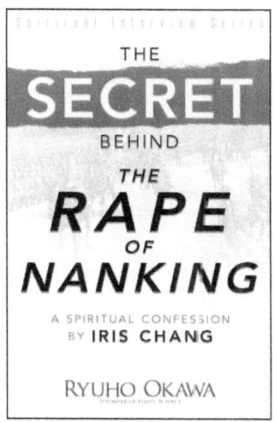

THE SECRET BEHIND
"THE RAPE OF NANKING"
A Spiritual Confession by Iris Chang

ISBN: 978-1-941779-08-8
$9.95 (Paperback)

Sometimes a single book can determine how the international society sees history, as well as give a great impact on international relations. If a fabricated history had spread throughout the world and is subjecting the citizens of a particular country to humiliation that they don't deserve, then speaking from international justice and humanitarian viewpoints, such history must be rewritten in an objective and impartial manner. There is a phrase, "History is written by the victors." The usual process is that, after a war, the victors come up with a one-sided historical view that is advantageous to them and historical researchers of later generations gradually make corrections to it.

Nevertheless, sometimes history takes a sudden turn due to revelations from Heaven. This book is a rare example of that. The author of a book which gave a great impact on the historical view that had spread throughout the international society today confessed the truth regarding the content of her book and its background, just 10 years after her death, in a form of a spiritual message.

THE GENIUS OF ICHIRO

The Secret Behind His Four Thousand Hits

ISBN: 978-1-941779-04-0
$14.95 (Paperback)

Ichiro Suzuki arrived in Seattle in 2001 as a mostly anonymous free agent from Japan's NPB, and while there was buzz about his potential, no one really knew what to expect. Since then, he has set many records in American Major League Baseball, including the record for most hits in a single season (262) and longest streak of two-hundred-hit seasons (ten years). On August 21, 2013, he got the four thousandth hit of his professional baseball career. This spiritual interview reveals the "making of Ichiro," including the secrets to his professionalism, his techniques for overcoming slumps, and how he made it to the top. The interview highlights Ichiro's unique traits that continue to impress us, twelve years after he first unleashed the laser beam.

ON HAPPINESS REVOLUTION

A Spiritual Interview with Hannah Arendt

ISBN: 978-1-937673-82-6

$14.95 (Paperback)

Since 2010, Master Ryuho Okawa has published over two hundred spiritual messages, in Japanese, from the spirits of historical men and women and the guardian spirits of today's living figures. With this Spiritual Interview Series, Master Okawa is now making these important messages available in English. The books in this series are messages from the spirits or guardian spirits of people who have a great deal of influence over world affairs. These messages reveal these powerful figures' hidden intentions and disclose facts that even news reporters would have difficulty drawing out. Master Okawa's in-depth analyses of these messages give us the tools that we need to understand and confront the dangers that lie ahead of us. Master Okawa hopes to show readers that the spirit world and spirits are real, and that by understanding spiritual truths, we can bring a peaceful end to international conflicts and create solutions to a variety of global crises.

ARE ISLAMIC EXTREMISTS
JIHADISTS OR TERRORISTS?
The Necessity of Freedom in Islamic Countries

ISBN: 978-1-941779-14-9
$14.95 (Paperback)

The West has been leading a long war on terror since the 9/11 terrorist attacks in 2001 on American soil by Osama bin Laden's al-Qaeda. Even after the assassination of Osama bin Laden on May 2, 2011, by President Obama's Special Forces unit, terrorist attacks have continued around the world. On January 16, 2013, an international crisis erupted when Islamic terrorists organized by Mokhtar Belmokhtar lay siege to an Algerian gas plant. After the Algerian government sent in a special forces unit, thirty-nine foreign hostages were killed and 685 Algerian workers and one hundred foreigners escaped or were freed. *

Are the attacks by Islamic extremist groups like al-Qaeda and the organization led by Mokhtar Belmokhtar unjust acts of terror? Or are they justified acts of a holy war, as the self-proclaimed jihadists claim? In this interview with Osama bin Laden, Master Ryuho Okawa provides us with his conclusive answer to these questions.

* "Q&A: Hostage Crisis in Algeria," BBC News, January 21, 2013, http://www.bbc.com/news/world-africa-21056884.

LEADERSHIP SECRETS OF LIU BANG

The Emperor of China's Han Dynasty
with a Surprising Connection with Steven Spielberg

ISBN: 978-1-941779-17-0
$14.95 (Paperback)

Liu Bang, also known as Gaozu, began from humble peasant roots and served as a police officer under the Qin dynasty. He rose through the ranks, first receiving control of western China, and eventually becoming the ruler of China as the founder and first emperor of the Han dynasty (206 BCE–220 CE). The histories of kings and rulers often provide valuable lessons about the universal principles that can be applied to today's management, entrepreneurship, and all types of large undertakings. As this spiritual interview has shown, Liu Bang's strengths and achievements are marked by a strong global element. Everyone who aspires to lead a large organization can learn from his ability to win people's hearts. You may be surprised to discover that this long-ago emperor of China is living today in the United States as one of the world's most famous film directors, Steven Spielberg.

THE TRUTH OF NANKING AND COMFORT WOMEN ISSUES

A Spiritual Reading into World War II
by Edgar Cayce

ISBN: 978-1-937673-86-4
$14.95 (Paperback)

Did the so-called "Nanking Massacre" and the military comfort women forcefully taken by the Japanese troops actually exist as historical facts? In this book, we attempt to investigate whether the two events actually took place by using a new method. This is not merely to restore the international honor of Japan. We are hoping to review the causes of World War II, look over the world justice made by the victorious nations after the war and reveal the true world history.

THE NEW DIPLOMATIC STRATEGIES OF SIR WINSTON CHURCHILL

A Spiritual Interview with the Former Prime Minister Regarding the Age
of Perseverance

ISBN: 978-1-937673-85-7
$14.95 (Paperback)

Today, two politicians are criticized and compared to Hitler;
President Vladimir Putin of Russia and Prime Minister Shinzo
Abe of Japan. Are these politicians really dangerous to be likened
to Hitler? Or, just like in Hitler's case, can it be that another truly
dangerous politician exists in another country that is yet to be
discovered? If there is a chance to hear the opinion of Sir Winston
Churchill, considered to be Hitler's arch enemy, journalists around
the world would probably be interested to hear this.

The series on Spiritual Messages by Ryuho Okawa, Happy Science,
made this possible. This book contains a record of an interview
conducted with the spirit of former British Prime Minister
Churchill by Master Okawa in March this year. It is a record of an
interview on issues related to the "next appearance of Hitler," and
on current international affairs.

THE ART OF BUSINESS REVITALIZATION

Management Wisdom from Jack Welch,
Carlos Ghosn, and Bill Gates

ISBN: 978-1-937673-70-3
$19.95 (Paperback)

In *The Art of Business Revitalization: Management Wisdom from Jack Welch*, Carlos Ghosn, and Bill Gates, Master Ryuho Okawa conducts spiritual interviews with three of the greatest executives of our time. General Electric's Jack Welch, Renault and Nissan's Carlos Ghosn, and Microsoft's Bill Gates give readers a glimpse into how they took hold of opportunities and turned them into successes. What management philosophies helped Jack Welch and Carlos Ghosn turn around their companies during downturns? What is Bill Gates's secret to creating products that become global standards? What human resources management and education philosophies have they drawn upon to keep their companies at the top? This book reveals the secrets to their achievements.

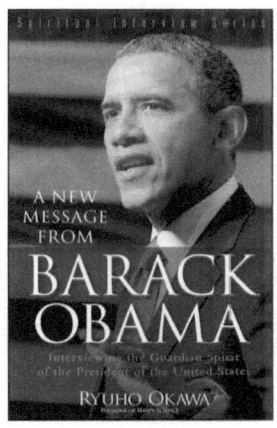

A NEW MESSAGE FROM
BARACK OBAMA

Interviewing the Guardian Spirit of
the President of the United States

ISBN: 978-1-937673-89-5
$14.95 (Paperback)

In April 2014, President Obama embarked on his fifth trip to Asia
during his time in office to discuss the pressing issues in the Asia-
pacific region. A week before his Asia trip, Master Ryuho Okawa
held a spiritual interview with Barack Obama, which revealed his true
objectives of his Asia tour and about his thoughts on current affairs
in the world. What is President Obama's vision of America's role in
the world today? Why does he believe that America is not the world's
policeman? This spiritual interview reveals President Obama's stance
on international relations including America's relationship with
China, the Ukraine crisis and Islamic extremism. It also discloses
his honest feelings about Japanese Prime Minister Abe and Russian
President Putin. Now that America is "on the verge of crisis," as the
guardian spirit of President Obama says in this interview, we all need
to think about how we can achieve security, justice and peace in the
world without the "world's policeman."

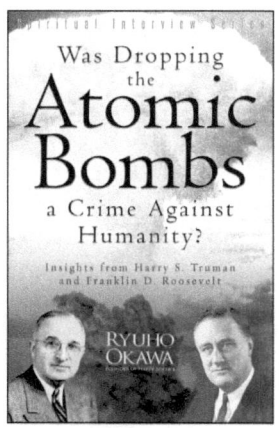

WAS DROPPING THE ATOMIC BOMBS A CRIME AGAINST HUMANITY?

Insights from Harry S. Truman
and Franklin D. Roosevelt

ISBN: 978-1-937673-78-9
$14.95 (Paperback)

Was there any true justification for the atomic bombing of Hiroshima and Nagasaki? To answer to this question, Master Ryuho Okawa conducted spiritual interviews with Harry S. Truman and Franklin D. Roosevelt, the two presidents who presided over the United States' participation in World War II. Could anything justify the use of nuclear weapons on civilians? Was Pearl Harbor really a sneak attack, or did Franklin Roosevelt know of it beforehand? This book reveals valuable information that will help the world gain a truthful understanding of world history.

JAPAN! REGAIN YOUR SAMURAI SPIRIT

A Message from the Guardian Spirit of Lee Teng-hui, Former President of the Republic of China

IISBN: 978-1-937673-77-2
$14.95 (Paperback)

This book is the record of interviews conducted on Former President of Taiwan Lee Teng-hui's subconscious [guardian spirit] in February 2014. His true thoughts, as well as the truth on modern East-Asian history, were revealed in these interviews. The book is filled with hints on how to give another thought to the causes of World War II. As it is stated in the afterword, this is a book which we want "all politicians, all people in the media, and everyone who talks about politics" to read.

DIPLOMATIC STRATEGY FOR JAPAN, U.S. AND CHINA
A Message from the Guardian Spirit of
Diplomatic Analyst Hisahiko Okazaki

ISBN: 978-1-937673-75-8
$14.95 (Paperback)

This book contains the interview conducted with the guardian spirit of former diplomat, Hisahiko Okazaki, a conservative commentator representative to Japan. An astonishing relation between Admiral Perry and Okazaki is revealed in this interview. By reading this book, you will come to know what Admiral Perry thinks on the current situation of the world, and the relation between Japan and the United States, 160 years later since he opened up Japan which was in seclusion.

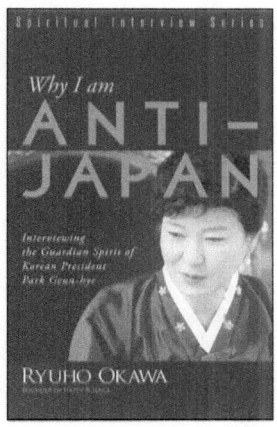

WHY I AM ANTI-JAPAN

Interviewing the Guardian Spirit of
Korean President Park Geun-hye

ISBN: 978-1-937673-67-3
$14.95 (Paperback)

This book is the record of interviews conducted on President Park's subconscious [guardian spirit] in February 2014, which were done in order to find out the fundamental reason to her anti-Japanese sentiments. Her true thoughts, as well as the truth on modern Japan-Korea history, were revealed in these interviews. By having numerous people in the world know of this truth, starting with the Japanese, South Koreans, Americans and the Chinese, the path to create a constructive future of the Pacific Basin should open as we resolve the conflicting emotions between Japan and South Korea in the international society.

A WARNING TO
SOUTH KOREA'S PRESIDENT

Words from Her Father,
Former President Park Chung-hee

ISBN: 978-1-937673-65-9
$14.95 (Paperback)

Park Chung-hee served as the president of the Republic of
Korea (South Korea) for almost sixteen years, from 1963 until
his death in 1979. Today, people around the world know him as
the assassinated father of Park Geun-hye, the current and first
female president of South Korea. In this spiritual interview, Park
Chung-hee's spirit shares his opinions on the roles of South
Korea, Japan, the United States, China, and North Korea in the
global context. What are his thoughts on the Takeshima island
dispute, the comfort-women issue, China's future prospects, and
the direction South Korea should take as a country? A Warning
to South Korea's President is a father's message to his daughter
as he seeks to guide their nation in the right direction. This
interview lets us see history in a new light and shows us how to
build a better future for the Asia-Pacific region.

INTERVIEWING THE GUARDIAN SPIRIT OF U.S. AMBASSADOR CAROLINE KENNEDY

A New Bridge between Japan and the U.S.

ISBN: 978-1-937673-63-5
$14.95 (Paperback)

CONTENTS
1 Caroline's Guardian Spirit Makes an "Informal" Appearance
2 Her View on Japan-U.S. and Japan-China Relations
3 True Emotions Behind America's Disappointment in Yasukuni Visit
4 World War II
5 Comfort Women Issue and Women's Rights
6 The Reason Behind the Kennedy Tragedies
7 Drive-Hunt Dolphin Killing, and Japanese vs. American Cultures
8 Japanese Princess and Roman Emperor in Past Lives?
9 Message to Japan

FOR THE FUTURE OF THAILAND AND JAPAN

Interviewing the Guardian Spirit of
Yingluck Shinawatra

ISBN: 978-1-937673-59-8
$14.95 (Paperback)

In December 2013, Thailand's Prime Minister Yingluck announced the dissolution of the nation's parliament and called a snap election to be held in February 2014. But this did not appease the thousands of angry protestors who remained on the streets of Bangkok.

During this time of social unrest, Prime Minister Yingluck were mostly absent from Bangkok to avoid protestors, spending more time in the Northern and Northeastern areas. It was in such a difficult time for the prime minister and the country of Thailand that Master Ryuho Okawa conducted a spiritual interview with Prime Minister Yingluck. In this spiritual interview, the guardian spirit of Prime Minister Yingluck shares her views on many controversial topics including democracy in Thailand, Thailand's relationships with China and Japan, traditional Buddhism, and Islam. She then asks Japan to help her country which has plunged into turmoil. It is Master Ryuho Okawa's hope that this interview will become a bridge to build a wonderful relationship between Thailand and Japan.

MOTHER TERESA'S CURRENT CALLING IN HEAVEN

The Saint of the Gutters Delivers Her Experiences of God,
Heaven, and Our Mission

ISBN: 978-1-937673-55-0
$14.95 (Paperback)

This book is a spiritual interview with Mother Teresa's spirit who talks through Master Ryuho Okawa. In this spiritual interview, which was conducted sixteen years after Mother Teresa's death, Mother Teresa's spirit talks about her astonishing discoveries about God, Heaven, and the mission that people on earth should aim to fulfill through life. Mother Teresa reveals that the other world is a vast place with many levels of angels, that Heaven and Hell exist, and that the reality of the human being is the soul. In addition to a discussion about the contradictions within Christian teachings and the need for new teachings for today's people, she also talks about her discoveries about God and Jesus Christ, and says that it is the mission of the wealthy to help others who are in poverty, through prayer and a pure heart.

NELSON MANDELA'S LAST MESSAGE

A Conversation with Madiba
Six Hours After His Death

ISBN: 978-1-937673-53-6
$14.95 (Paperback)

On December 5, 2013, the entire world mourned the passing of Nelson Mandela. Even as the news was spreading, Mandela's spirit came to Master Ryuho Okawa to give us all an important message of hope and to prove that the afterlife exists. Archbishop of Canterbury Justin Wilby paid this tribute to the first black president of South Africa and the man who liberated his country from apartheid: "His courage was undefeated, indomitable, extraordinary." Perhaps it was Mandela's indomitable belief in the fundamental reality of the human soul that gave him such extraordinary courage in the face of adversity. For as he says in this spiritual interview, God created our souls as thinking energy without color, and that our colorless soul is the basis of our fundamental freedom and equality. In this spiritual interview, Master Ryuho Okawa gives us a glimpse into the mind of this great leader whose undefeated spirit is a message of hope to us all.

SOUTH KOREA'S CONSPIRACY

President Park's Hidden Agenda to Unite with China

ISBN: 978-1-937673-51-2
$14.95 (Paperback)

On June 27, 2013, South Korea's President Park Geun-hye and Chinese President Xi Jinping held summit talks in Beijing. At the meeting, President Park asked China's Xi Jinping to build a memorial of An Jung-geun, the man who in 1909 assassinated the first Prime Minister of Japan and the first Resident-General of Korea, Ito Hirobumi. In this spiritual interview, we begin by speaking with the spirit of An Jung-geun before moving on to a conversation with the guardian spirit of President Park, who forced herself into the interview out of fear that the interview will reveal the truth about him. Through these conversations, Master Ryuho Okawa tries to discover the facts about the assassination of Ito Hirobumi to determine whether An Jung-geun can justifiably be hailed as a hero. While South Koreans continue to accuse Japan of having wronged their nation, Master Okawa hopes that these interviews will provide a truthful understanding of the historical events between Japan and South Korea and help the international community understand the nature of true international justice.

MARGARET THATCHER'S
MIRACULOUS MESSAGE

An Interview with the Iron Lady
19 Hours After Her Death

ISBN: 978-1-937673-37-6
$14.95 (Paperback)

On April 9, 2013, just nineteen hours after Margaret Thatcher's death, Master Ryuho Okawa summoned her spirit to hold a miraculous spiritual interview with Europe's first female prime minister, famously known as the Iron Lady. In words marked by her signature clarity and determination, Margaret Thatcher provided valuable answers to essential and timely questions. Her answers will prove helpful not only to the United Kingdom, but also to the global economy and governments all over the world, including those of the United States and the European Union.

UNMASKING BAN KI-MOON'S
BIASED STANCE

Investigating the Paralysis of the United Nations

ISBN: 978-1-937673-49-9
$14.95 (Paperback)

The world is currently facing many critical international issues that require resolution through strong leadership dedicated to the preservation of international peace and security. What are U.N. Secretary-General Ban Ki-moon's true thoughts on these pressing issues? What does he think about the disputes between Japan and South Korea over ownership of the Takeshima Islands, between Japan and China over ownership of the Senkaku Islands, and between Iran and Israel over nuclear weapons capability? Can we depend on him to successfully uphold the principle of impartiality in the United Nations's role of peacemaking? In this spiritual interview with the guardian spirit of Mr. Ban Ki-moon, Master Okawa reveals the U.N. Secretary-General's true character and true intentions regarding his important peacemaking responsibilities.

STEVE JOBS RETURNS
WITH HIS SECRETS

Be Simple, Be Crazy

ISBN: 978-1-937673-47-5
$19.95 (Paperback)

In this spiritual interview with Steve Jobs, conducted just three months after his death, Master Okawa offers us a chance to catch a glimpse into the mind of one of America's modern geniuses, whom President Barack Obama has described as one among the greatest American innovators. What was the aesthetic philosophy behind his passionate drive to create products that he described as "at the intersection of art and technology?" What were the secrets to his creativity and the successful sales of his products? As Master Okawa often says, and as this interview with the mind of one of the greatest modern innovators will show you, success is always in the way we think and in the substance of our goals and ideals.

THE SYRIAN CRISIS

What Is God's Verdict on U.S. Military Intervention?

ISBN: 978-1-937673-44-4
$14.95 (Paperback)

Is there justice in a U.S. military intervention into the ongoing Syrian crisis? What is God's perspective on the tragedy that is occurring in Syria? In *The Syrian Crisis: What Is God's Verdict on U.S. Military Intervention?* Master Ryuho Okawa conducts a spiritual interview with the guardian spirit of Bashar al-Assad. As this interview reveals, the Syrian dictator's true character is quite different from what we saw in the CBS interview. As the world braces for a possible world war, Master Ryuho Okawa provides us with a clear sense of where God's justice lies in this international crisis.

THE JUST CAUSE IN THE IRAQ WAR

Did Saddam Hussein Possess
Weapons of Mass Destruction?

ISBN: 978-1-937673-41-3
$14.95 (Paperback)

The Just Cause in the Iraq War: Did Saddam Hussein Possess Weapons of Mass Destruction? tackles one of the most controversial and pertinent issues in international politics today. Is President Obama correct that the Iraq War was an unjust war, as he claimed during the 2012 presidential race? Did Saddam Hussein truly have no weapons of mass destruction, or are those weapons still hidden in Iraq, somewhere beyond the reach of U.S. intelligence? In this book, you will discover that Saddam Hussein was also behind the planning of the 9/11 terrorist attacks and both he and Osama bin Laden are now in Hell. The knowledge this book provides will help each of us make the right decisions as we work together to create a peaceful international society.

FORECASTING THE SECOND KOREAN WAR

How Will the World Handle the Crisis?

ISBN: 978-1-937673-35-2
$14.95 (Paperback)

Forecasting the Second Korean War: How Will the World Handle the Crisis? forecasts a potential crisis that the United States, South Korea, and Japan may face. In part 1, Master Okawa draws on the help of Edgar Cayce to describe in detail the unfolding of a second Korean War that could begin in the summer of 2013. Part 2 of this book contains a spiritual interview with Kim Il Sung that reveals that he is spiritually guiding Kim Jong Un. Together, the two parts of this book reveal the shocking fact that the crisis on the Korean peninsula is only a small part of a larger and more global imperialistic scheme that is being masterminded by Xi Jinping, the president of China. You will discover who is truly behind the Islamist terrorist attacks against the United States.

EXPOSING NORTH KOREA'S MENACING LEADER

Kim Jong Un's Plot for a Psychological War

ISBN: 978-1-937673-39-0
$14.95 (Paperback)

Exposing North Korea's Menacing Leader: Kim Jong Un's Plot for a Psychological War reveals the role that North Korea is playing in China's imperialistic strategy and the two nations' close ties with Iran. Together, China and Kim Jong Un—North Korea's supreme leader— are carrying out a psychological war that takes full advantage of the weaknesses of Japanese Prime Minister Abe and United States President Obama. Indeed, this interview with Kim Jong Un's guardian spirit reveals that Kim Jong Un was most likely behind the Boston marathon bombings that occurred on April 15, 2013.

THE IRAN-ISRAEL CRISIS

Looking for a Way to Prevent a Nuclear War

ISBN: 978-1-937673-26-0
$14.95 (Paperback)

Master Ryuho Okawa firmly believes that the power to create lasting global peace will come from embracing love and forgiveness beyond differences in religion. This set of spiritual interviews with the guardian spirits of Iran's President Mahmoud Ahmadinejad and Israel's Prime Minister Benjamin Netanyahu reveal their living counterparts' underlying ideas about each other's nations as arch enemies. You will discover hints to solving long-standing clashes between religions.

CHINA'S SECRET MILITARY BASES

A Remote-Viewing Investigation
of Suspicious Satellite Images

ISBN: 978-1-937673-24-6
$14.95 (Paperback)

Master Okawa reveals China's versions of Area 51 from mysterious satellite photos that had aroused worldwide curiosity. Even American intelligence will be shocked to find out these truths about a hidden enormous missile-launching site full of nuclear warheads prepared to strike major cities around the world. This book is a must-read for anyone who wants to save the world from a full-out nuclear war.

HAVE FAITH IN GREAT AMERICA
Liberty and World Justice for All

ISBN: 978-1-937673-20-8
$14.95 (Paperback)

Have Faith in Great America: Liberty and World Justice for All is Master Ryuho Okawa's earnest message to the United States of America. The world's future depends on America's fulfillment of its long-held sacred mission of protecting the faith, liberty, and justice of people and nations around the world, and on the development of strong bonds between the United States and Japan.

CHINA'S HIDDEN AGENDA
The Mastermind Behind the Anti-American
and Anti-Japanese Protests

ISBN: 978-1937673-18-5
$14.95 (Paperback)

"Anti-American demonstrations have been raging in over twenty Arab countries. The man pulling the strings behind all this is Xi Jinping."

—Master Ryuho Okawa

"I wanted to stir up the anti-American movement in the Arab world to make sure that the United States won't be able to attack Syria or Iran...I'm the mastermind behind the Muhammad video."

—Xi Jinping's Guardian Spirit

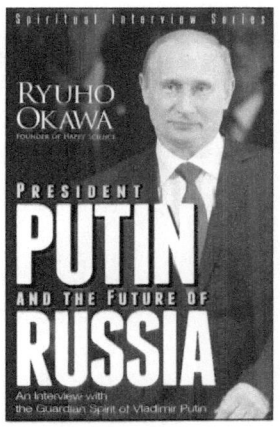

PRESIDENT PUTIN AND
THE FUTURE OF RUSSIA

An Interview with the Guardian Spirit
of Vladimir Putin

ISBN: 978-1-937673-14-7
$14.95 (Paperback)

"I have no intention of fighting the United States. The Cold War is over... I have no intention of fighting the Americans... And I'm not friendly enough with China to think about joining them against the United States... I have given Russians religious freedom, which makes me very different from the Chinese."

—Putin's Guardian Spirit